THE ORIGIN AND EVOLUTION OF COMPUTERS

Shreyan Hait

GodDevil Books

Dedication

To the pioneers and visionaries of computing, whose relentless curiosity, ingenuity, and perseverance have transformed the world.

To Charles Babbage, Ada Lovelace, Alan Turing, John von Neumann, and the countless other innovators who laid the foundations for modern technology.

To the engineers, programmers, and dreamers who brought the impossible to life, and to those who continue to push the boundaries of what is possible.

This book is dedicated to you, for your contributions have not only changed the course of history but have also inspired generations to dream bigger and reach further.

And to my family and friends, for your unwavering support and encouragement throughout this journey.

Thank you.

"I think it's fair to say that personal computers have become the most empowering tool we've ever created. They're tools of communication, they're tools of creativity, and they can be shaped by their user."

BILL GATES

CONTENTS

PREFACE

The journey of computing is one of the most fascinating narratives in the history of human innovation. From the humble beginnings of mechanical calculation devices to the complex and interconnected digital world we live in today, the evolution of computers has profoundly transformed every aspect of our lives. This book, "The Origin and Evolution of Computers," seeks to chronicle this remarkable journey, exploring the milestones, inventions, and visionary individuals that have shaped the field of computing.

My interest in the history of computers began as a curiosity about the devices that have become so integral to our daily routines. How did we progress from simple counting tools to sophisticated machines capable of processing vast amounts of data in the blink of an eye? What were the pivotal moments and key breakthroughs that set us on this path? And who were the pioneers whose vision and perseverance brought these ideas to life?

In writing this book, I aimed to provide a comprehensive yet accessible account of computing history. Each chapter is dedicated to a specific era or technological leap, offering detailed insights into the development and impact of various innovations. From the early mechanical devices and the pioneering work of Charles Babbage and Ada Lovelace to the advent of electronic computers and the revolutionary rise of the microprocessor, this book covers a wide array of topics that collectively narrate the story of computing.

One of the most exciting aspects of this narrative is the human element. The history of computers is not just about machines and technology but also about the people behind them. Visionaries like Alan Turing, John von Neumann, Bill Gates, Steve Jobs, and many others played crucial roles in advancing the field. Their stories are interwoven with the technical developments, providing a richer context and deeper understanding of how and why these advancements occurred.

The impact of computers on society cannot be overstated. They have revolutionized industries, transformed economies, and reshaped the way we interact with the world and each other. This book also delves into these broader implications, examining how computers have influenced everything from business and government to education, healthcare, and our daily lives.

As we look to the future, the pace of technological change shows no signs of slowing down. Emerging fields such as artificial intelligence, quantum computing, and the Internet of Things promise to usher in new waves of innovation and transformation. Understanding the history of computers not only provides a foundation for appreciating these future developments but also offers valuable lessons and insights.

I hope this book serves as an informative and engaging guide to the history of computers. Whether you are a student, a technology enthusiast, or simply someone interested in understanding the tools that have become so central to modern life, I trust you will find the journey through these pages both enlightening and inspiring.

Thank you for embarking on this journey with me.

[Shreyan Hait]
[20-05-2024]

INTRODUCTION

The history of computers is a fascinating journey through time, marked by extraordinary innovations and groundbreaking advancements that have fundamentally transformed our world. From the earliest mechanical devices to the powerful and ubiquitous digital machines of today, the evolution of computing technology reflects human ingenuity and the relentless pursuit of progress.

This book, "The Origin and Evolution of Computers," aims to take you on a chronological voyage through the milestones and pivotal moments that have defined the field of computing. Each chapter explores a distinct era, highlighting the key inventions, influential figures, and significant breakthroughs that have shaped the trajectory of modern technology.

We begin our journey with the dawn of computing, where early civilizations devised rudimentary tools to aid in arithmetic and record-keeping. These primitive devices, like the abacus, laid the foundational concepts that would later evolve into more complex mechanical calculators.

As we move forward, we delve into the work of visionary pioneers such as Charles Babbage and Ada Lovelace, whose conceptual designs of programmable machines in the 19th century foreshadowed the digital age. Their theoretical contributions provided a crucial stepping stone for the scientific and engineering advancements that followed.

The early 20th century brought a new wave of innovation with the advent of electronic computers. The development of machines like the ENIAC and UNIVAC marked a significant leap from mechanical to electronic computing, introducing unprecedented speed and reliability. This era also saw the rise of mainframe computers, which became the backbone of business and government operations, enabling large-scale data processing and complex calculations.

The microprocessor revolution of the 1970s was a turning point, democratizing computing power and leading to the creation of personal computers. Companies like Apple, IBM, and Microsoft played pivotal roles in this transformation, making computers accessible to individuals and small businesses and sparking a wave of technological innovation that continues to this day.

As we enter the digital age, the interconnected world of the Internet and networking has reshaped how we communicate, work, and live. The advent of portable computing devices, such as laptops, tablets, and smartphones, has further integrated technology into our daily lives, making information and connectivity available at our fingertips.

In the modern era, advancements in artificial intelligence, cloud computing, and quantum computing are pushing the boundaries of what is possible, promising to revolutionize industries and society once again. This book also explores the social and cultural impacts of these technologies, addressing issues of accessibility, ethics, and privacy in an increasingly digital world.

Finally, we reflect on the lessons learned from this remarkable journey and consider the future directions and potential innovations that may shape the next chapters in the story of computing.

"The Origin and Evolution of Computers" is not just a technical account of machines and systems; it is a tribute to the creative minds and relentless innovators who have driven the field forward. It is a story of human achievement, vision, and the ever-evolving quest to harness the power of computation to solve problems, enhance lives, and unlock new possibilities.

We invite you to join us on this journey through time, exploring the rich history and exciting future of computers. Whether you are a seasoned technologist, a curious student, or simply an enthusiast of technological history, this book offers insights and inspiration from the remarkable evolution of one of humanity's most transformative inventions.

FOREWORD

In the ever-evolving landscape of technology, understanding the history of computing is essential for appreciating the present and envisioning the future. "The Origin and Evolution of Computers" offers readers a captivating journey through the milestones, innovations, and individuals that have shaped the modern computing landscape.

As a technologist with a passion for innovation and progress, I am delighted to see this comprehensive exploration of computing history. From the earliest mechanical devices to the emergence of electronic computers, the microprocessor revolution, and the advent of the Internet age, this book provides a rich tapestry of insights into how we arrived at our current technological state.

What sets this book apart is its focus on the human stories behind the technology. It is not merely a recounting of technical achievements but a celebration of the visionaries, inventors, and trailblazers who dared to imagine a world transformed by computing. From the pioneering work of Charles Babbage and Ada Lovelace to the entrepreneurial spirit of Bill Gates and Steve Jobs, each chapter is enriched by the personal narratives of those who shaped the course of computing history.

Furthermore, "The Origin and Evolution of Computers" does not shy away from exploring the broader societal impacts of computing. It examines how computers have revolutionized industries, empowered individuals, and reshaped the way we live, work, and communicate. By providing this holistic perspective, the book encourages readers to consider the ethical, social, and philosophical dimensions of technology in addition to its technical prowess.

As we stand on the cusp of an era defined by artificial intelligence, quantum computing, and the Internet of Things, understanding the lessons of computing history has never been more critical. This book serves as a valuable resource for anyone seeking to navigate the complexities of our digital age with insight and foresight.

I commend the author for their dedication to documenting this fascinating journey through computing history. Whether you are a seasoned technologist, an aspiring innovator, or simply a curious mind eager to explore the wonders of technology, "The Origin and Evolution of Computers" promises to inform, inspire, and enlighten.

Let us embark on this journey together, embracing the past, present, and future of computing with curiosity and optimism.

[Shreyan Hait]
[20-05-2024]

PROLOGUE

In the quiet solitude of a dusty workshop, a visionary tinkers with gears, levers, and mechanical contraptions, dreaming of a machine that can perform complex calculations with precision and speed. In another corner of the world, a mathematician sketches diagrams and algorithms on paper, envisioning a device that can process symbols and execute instructions with the elegance of thought itself. These disparate visions, born of curiosity and imagination, are the seeds from which the modern computer would eventually emerge.

"The Origin and Evolution of Computers" begins not with silicon chips and digital circuits but with the dreams and aspirations of those who dared to imagine a world transformed by technology. From the earliest civilizations that devised primitive counting tools to the brilliant minds of the 20th century who brought electronic computers to life, this book traces the arc of human ingenuity and innovation across millennia.

As we embark on this journey, we will encounter the towering figures who shaped the course of computing history: Charles Babbage, the father of the mechanical computer; Ada Lovelace, the visionary mathematician who foresaw the potential of programmable machines; Alan

Turing, the codebreaker whose insights laid the foundation for modern computing; and countless others whose names may be less familiar but whose contributions were no less significant.

We will witness the birth of electronic computers, marveling at the sheer scale and complexity of machines like the ENIAC and UNIVAC that paved the way for the digital revolution. We will explore the microprocessor revolution, which brought computing power to the masses and forever changed the way we interact with technology. And we will delve into the emergence of the Internet and networking, which connected the world in ways that were once unimaginable.

But this is not just a story of machines and circuits; it is a story of human endeavor and the relentless pursuit of progress. It is a testament to the boundless creativity and resilience of the human spirit, and a reminder that the greatest achievements are often born of humble beginnings and audacious dreams.

As we journey through the pages of this book, let us celebrate the pioneers and visionaries who have shaped the world of computing. Let us marvel at the ingenuity and innovation that have propelled us from the abacus to the smartphone, from the punch card to the cloud. And let us reflect on the lessons of history as we chart a course toward an ever more interconnected and technologically advanced future.

Welcome to "The Origin and Evolution of Computers." May this journey inspire you to imagine, innovate, and explore the limitless possibilities of the digital age.

[Shreyan Hait]
[20-05-2024]

CHAPTER 1: THE DAWN OF COMPUTING

Introduction to Early Computing Concepts

The story of computing begins long before the digital age, with humankind's quest to solve complex problems and perform calculations more efficiently. Early civilizations devised various tools and methods to aid in arithmetic, marking the first steps toward automated computation. These primitive tools laid the groundwork for future technological advancements.

One of the earliest known computing devices is the **abacus**, which dates back to ancient Mesopotamia around 2400 BCE. The abacus, with its rows of beads on rods, allowed users to perform basic arithmetic operations such as addition, subtraction, multiplication, and division. Variations of the abacus were developed in different cultures, including the Chinese suanpan and the Roman abacus, highlighting its universal appeal and effectiveness.

As time progressed, the need for more sophisticated computational tools became apparent, especially in fields like astronomy, navigation, and engineering. This need spurred the development of more complex mechanical devices.

Abacuses and Early Mechanical Devices

In the 17th century, the landscape of computation began to change significantly. Inventors and mathematicians sought to create machines that could perform calculations more quickly and accurately than manual methods. Among the earliest pioneers was **Blaise Pascal**, a French mathematician who, in 1642, invented the Pascaline—a mechanical calculator capable of performing addition and subtraction. The Pascaline utilized a series of gears and wheels, representing a significant leap forward in mechanical computation.

Shortly after Pascal, the German polymath **Gottfried Wilhelm Leibniz** advanced the field further with his invention of the **Leibniz Wheel** in 1673. This device could perform all four basic arithmetic operations, including multiplication and division, by using a stepped drum mechanism. Leibniz's work laid crucial theoretical foundations for binary arithmetic, which would become central to modern computing.

Despite these advancements, the true visionary of early computing was **Charles Babbage**, an English mathematician and inventor. Often referred to as the "father of the computer," Babbage conceptualized machines that went far beyond basic arithmetic calculations.

Charles Babbage and the Analytical Engine

In the early 19th century, Charles Babbage embarked on an ambitious project to design a machine that could perform not just arithmetic operations but also more complex calculations automatically. His first major project, the **Difference Engine,** aimed to automate the production of mathematical tables, which were crucial for fields like astronomy and navigation. Though he encountered significant engineering challenges and funding issues, Babbage's work on the Difference Engine demonstrated the potential of mechanical computation.

Babbage's most groundbreaking idea, however, was the **Analytical Engine**. Conceived in 1837, the Analytical Engine was a mechanical general-purpose computer. It featured key elements of modern computers, including a **mill** (analogous to a CPU), a **store** (memory), and the ability to use punched cards to input programs and data. Babbage's vision for the Analytical Engine included conditional branching and loops, which are fundamental concepts in modern programming.

Although the Analytical Engine was never completed during Babbage's lifetime, his design was meticulously detailed and inspired future generations of computer scientists. Notably, **Ada Lovelace**, an English mathematician and writer, worked closely with Babbage. Lovelace's notes on the Analytical Engine included what is considered the first algorithm intended for implementation on a machine, earning her recognition as the world's first computer programmer.

Conclusion

The dawn of computing was marked by remarkable innovations from visionaries like Blaise Pascal, Gottfried Wilhelm Leibniz, Charles Babbage, and Ada Lovelace. Their pioneering work laid the theoretical and practical foundations for the development of modern computers. While their machines were mechanical and limited in scope, they embodied the fundamental principles of automated computation and foreshadowed the digital revolution to come.

As we move forward in our exploration of computing history, we will see how these early ideas evolved and were built upon by subsequent inventors and engineers, ultimately leading to the creation of the electronic computers that transformed the world.

CHAPTER 2: PIONEERS OF THE MODERN COMPUTER

Alan Turing and the Turing Machine

The early 20th century saw remarkable theoretical advancements that laid the groundwork for modern computers. Among the most significant contributors was **Alan Turing**, a British mathematician and logician whose work during the 1930s and 1940s profoundly influenced computer science.

In 1936, Turing introduced the concept of the **Turing Machine** in his seminal paper "On Computable Numbers, with an Application to the Entscheidungsproblem." The Turing Machine was an abstract mathematical model that defined the fundamental principles of computation. It consisted of an infinite tape divided into cells, a read-write head that could move left or right, and a set of rules (a program) for manipulating symbols on the tape. Turing demonstrated that his machine could simulate the logic of any computer algorithm, establishing the theoretical foundation for what we now understand as universal computation.

The Turing Machine was a profound breakthrough because it provided a formal definition of what it means for a function to be computable. This concept is central to computer science, as it delineates the limits of what can be achieved with any computational device. Turing's work also paved the way for the development of stored-program computers, where instructions and data are treated alike and can be modified during execution.

Konrad Zuse and the Z3

While Turing was laying the theoretical groundwork, **Konrad Zuse**, a German engineer, was building practical computing machines. In 1941, Zuse completed the **Z3**, which is considered the world's first fully operational programmable computer. The Z3 was a remarkable achievement, especially given the context of wartime Germany, where resources were scarce.

The Z3 used electromechanical relays and was capable of performing floating-point arithmetic. Its programmability was achieved through punched film, which allowed users to input instructions and data. Despite its mechanical nature, the Z3 embodied many features of modern computers, such as the ability to branch conditionally. Zuse's innovations went largely unrecognized outside Germany during the war, but his contributions were critical in the evolution of computing.

The Colossus and Codebreaking

During World War II, the development of computers accelerated due to the urgent need for codebreaking and other military applications. One of the most significant achievements of this era was the **Colossus**, a series of machines designed to decrypt German communications encoded with the Lorenz cipher.

Developed by a team led by **Tommy Flowers** at Bletchley Park in the United Kingdom, the first Colossus was operational by 1944. It used thousands of vacuum tubes, making it one of the earliest electronic digital computers. Colossus could read encrypted messages at high speeds, significantly aiding the Allied war effort by providing crucial intelligence.

The success of Colossus demonstrated the power of electronic computing and set the stage for post-war advancements. Although the project was shrouded in secrecy for many years, its legacy is now recognized as a pivotal moment in the history of computing.

Conclusion

The pioneering work of Alan Turing, Konrad Zuse, and the team behind Colossus marked a turning point in the development of computers. Turing's theoretical insights established the conceptual framework for universal computation, while Zuse's and Flowers' practical implementations showcased the potential of programmable and electronic machines.

These early efforts laid the foundation for the rapid advancements that would follow in the post-war era, leading to the creation of the first generation of electronic digital computers. As we continue our journey through the history of computing, we will see how these foundational concepts and early machines evolved, leading to the modern computers that have become integral to our lives.

CHAPTER 3: THE BIRTH OF ELECTRONIC COMPUTERS

The ENIAC and the Birth of the Modern Computer

The development of electronic computers began to gain momentum during and immediately after World War II. One of the most significant milestones in this era was the creation of the **ENIAC (Electronic Numerical Integrator and Computer)**, which marked a revolutionary step in computing technology.

John Presper Eckert and **John W. Mauchly,** engineers at the University of Pennsylvania, spearheaded the development of the ENIAC. Completed in 1945 and fully operational by 1946, ENIAC was the first general-purpose electronic digital computer. Unlike earlier mechanical and electromechanical machines, ENIAC used vacuum tubes to perform calculations, vastly increasing its speed and reliability.

ENIAC could perform complex calculations far more quickly than any previous machine, handling up to 5,000 operations per second. It was designed initially for artillery trajectory calculations for the U.S. Army but was later used for various scientific computations, including hydrogen bomb simulations and weather predictions.

One of ENIAC's major innovations was its programmability. Although reprogramming required manually setting switches and plugging and unplugging cables, it could be configured to solve a wide array of problems. This flexibility, combined with its electronic speed, made ENIAC a true forerunner of modern computers.

The Development of UNIVAC

Following the success of ENIAC, Eckert and Mauchly continued their work on electronic computers, leading to the development of the **UNIVAC I (UNIVersal Automatic Computer I)**. Completed in 1951, UNIVAC I was the first commercial computer produced in the United States and the first designed for business and administrative use, not just scientific calculations.

UNIVAC I featured several advancements over ENIAC. It used magnetic tape for input and output, which was more efficient than the punched cards used by earlier machines. It also had a much more sophisticated and user-friendly programming system. UNIVAC I's ability to handle both numerical and alphabetical data made it suitable for a wide range of applications, from census data processing to business accounting.

One of UNIVAC's most famous moments came in 1952 when it successfully predicted the outcome of the U.S.

presidential election, demonstrating the practical potential of electronic computers to a wide audience.

Early Transistor Computers

The transition from vacuum tubes to transistors marked another significant advancement in the evolution of computers. Transistors, invented in 1947 by **John Bardeen, Walter Brattain,** and **William Shockley** at Bell Laboratories, offered numerous advantages over vacuum tubes. They were smaller, more reliable, consumed less power, and generated less heat.

The first computers to use transistors began to appear in the late 1950s. One notable example was the **IBM 7090**, introduced in 1959. The IBM 7090 was one of the earliest fully transistorized computers and was widely used in scientific, engineering, and commercial applications. Its performance and reliability made it a popular choice for various large-scale computing tasks, including space missions and military simulations.

The use of transistors dramatically increased the speed and efficiency of computers, paving the way for further miniaturization and the development of more powerful and versatile machines.

Conclusion

The birth of electronic computers was characterized by rapid technological advancements and the transition from mechanical and electromechanical devices to fully electronic systems. The development of ENIAC, UNIVAC I, and early transistor computers demonstrated the immense potential of electronic computing and laid the foundation for the modern computer industry.

These early machines showcased the advantages of electronic components, programmability, and the ability to handle a diverse range of tasks. As we move forward in our exploration of computing history, we will see how these innovations evolved into the powerful and ubiquitous computers that have transformed our world.

The next chapters will delve into the era of mainframes, the microprocessor revolution, and the rise of personal computing, highlighting the continuous evolution and impact of these remarkable machines.

CHAPTER 4: THE AGE OF MAINFRAMES

IBM and the Dominance of Mainframes

The 1950s and 1960s heralded the rise of mainframe computers, large and powerful machines that became the backbone of business, government, and research institutions. Leading the charge in this era was **IBM (International Business Machines Corporation)**, which dominated the mainframe market and set industry standards that influenced computing for decades.

IBM's journey into mainframes began with the **IBM 701**, introduced in 1952 as the company's first commercial scientific computer. It was soon followed by the IBM 702, designed for business applications. These early successes paved the way for the iconic **IBM 704**, which introduced the concept of a standardized, mass-produced computer. The IBM 704 was notable for its use of magnetic core memory and support for high-level programming languages like Fortran, which significantly simplified the programming process and broadened the machine's appeal.

In 1964, IBM unveiled the **System/360**, a groundbreaking family of mainframe computers that could run the same software across a range of models with varying performance levels. This concept of compatibility revolutionized the industry by protecting users' investments in software and training. The System/360's modular design allowed businesses to upgrade their hardware without having to replace their entire computing infrastructure. This versatility and forward-thinking design ensured the System/360's dominance and solidified IBM's position as the leading mainframe manufacturer.

The Role of Mainframes in Business and Government

Mainframe computers quickly became indispensable in business and government due to their unparalleled processing power, reliability, and ability to handle large volumes of data. Corporations used mainframes for critical applications such as payroll processing, inventory management, and financial transactions. Banks, for instance, relied on mainframes to manage accounts, process transactions, and ensure data integrity, laying the groundwork for modern electronic banking.

Government agencies also harnessed the power of mainframes for tasks like census data processing, tax collection, and public administration. The ability to process vast amounts of data quickly and accurately made mainframes essential tools for large-scale operations and complex problem-solving.

One of the key advantages of mainframes was their capacity for **time-sharing**, a method that allowed multiple users to access the computer simultaneously. This innovation increased efficiency and maximized the utilization of computing resources, making mainframes more cost-effective and accessible to a broader range of users.

Advances in Data Storage and Processing

The age of mainframes saw significant advancements in data storage and processing technologies, further enhancing their capabilities. Magnetic tape, used for data storage and backup, evolved to provide higher storage capacities and faster access times. The introduction of **magnetic disk storage**, exemplified by IBM's **RAMAC 305** in 1956, marked a major leap forward. Disk storage offered random access to data, dramatically improving the speed and flexibility of data retrieval compared to sequential tape storage.

Mainframes also saw the development of sophisticated operating systems and database management systems (DBMS). **IBM's OS/360**, released in conjunction with the System/360, was one of the first operating systems to manage complex job scheduling, resource allocation, and data storage. Similarly, the emergence of DBMS, such as IBM's **IMS (Information Management System)**, enabled efficient organization, retrieval, and manipulation of large datasets, supporting more complex and dynamic applications.

Conclusion

The age of mainframes was characterized by rapid technological innovation and the establishment of computing standards that shaped the industry for years to come. IBM's leadership in developing powerful, reliable, and scalable mainframe systems played a crucial role in transforming how businesses and governments operated. The mainframe era laid the foundation for the data-driven world we live in today, proving the potential of computers to revolutionize multiple sectors.

As we continue our exploration of computing history, the next chapters will delve into the microprocessor revolution, which democratized computing power and led to the advent of personal computers. This transition marked a significant shift from the centralized, large-scale mainframe systems to more accessible and versatile computing devices, setting the stage for the digital age.

CHAPTER 5: THE MICROPROCESSOR REVOLUTION

The Invention of the Microprocessor

The early 1970s witnessed a transformative breakthrough in computing technology with the invention of the microprocessor. This single-chip integration of a computer's central processing unit (CPU) revolutionized the industry, making powerful computing capabilities accessible on a much smaller and more affordable scale.

The world's first commercially available microprocessor was the **Intel 4004**, introduced in 1971 by Intel Corporation. Designed by engineers **Federico Faggin** , **Ted Hoff**, and **Stanley Mazor**, the Intel 4004 was originally created for a Japanese calculator company, Busicom. This 4-bit microprocessor contained 2,300 transistors and could perform approximately 92,000 operations per second. Although modest by today's standards, the 4004 demonstrated the potential of microprocessors to revolutionize computing by significantly reducing size and cost.

Following the 4004, Intel quickly developed more

advanced microprocessors, including the **Intel 8008** in 1972 and the **Intel 8080** in 1974. The 8080, an 8-bit microprocessor, became particularly influential as it was powerful enough to run a computer on its own and was adopted in numerous early personal computers and embedded systems.

The Rise of Personal Computers

The advent of the microprocessor paved the way for the personal computer (PC) revolution, which brought computing power to homes and small businesses for the first time. One of the earliest and most iconic personal computers was the **Altair 8800**, released in 1975 by MITS (Micro Instrumentation and Telemetry Systems). Based on the Intel 8080 microprocessor, the Altair 8800 was sold as a kit that hobbyists could assemble. Its popularity spurred interest and innovation in the budding personal computing market.

Following the Altair 8800, companies like Apple, Commodore, and Tandy entered the market with their own personal computers. In 1976, **Steve Jobs** and **Steve Wozniak** introduced the **Apple I**, followed by the highly successful **Apple II** in 1977. The Apple II featured a user-friendly interface, color graphics, and expandable memory, making it appealing to a wide audience and establishing Apple as a major player in the personal computer industry.

Another significant milestone came in 1981 when IBM introduced the **IBM PC (Model 5150)**. Powered by the Intel 8088 microprocessor and running Microsoft's MS-DOS operating system, the IBM PC set a standard for hardware compatibility and software development that many other companies followed. The IBM PC's open architecture allowed third-party manufacturers to create compatible peripherals and software, fostering a rapidly growing ecosystem and solidifying the personal computer's place in both business and home environments.

Key Players: Apple, IBM, and Microsoft

Several key companies emerged as leaders during the microprocessor revolution, each playing a crucial role in shaping the personal computing landscape.

Apple Computer, Inc. (now Apple Inc.) became synonymous with innovation and design excellence in personal computing. The introduction of the **Macintosh** in 1984 further cemented Apple's reputation. The Macintosh featured a graphical user interface (GUI) and a mouse, making it much more accessible and user-friendly than command-line interfaces. These features were inspired by the pioneering work at Xerox PARC (Palo Alto Research Center), which developed many of the concepts later popularized by Apple.

IBM was instrumental in establishing the personal computer as a business tool. The success of the IBM PC and its subsequent models led to widespread adoption in corporate environments, ensuring that personal computers became essential office equipment. IBM's decision to use off-the-shelf components and open architecture encouraged a thriving market of compatible hardware and software, which helped lower costs and expand the market.

Microsoft emerged as a key software provider, initially by supplying the operating system for the IBM PC. **Bill Gates** and **Paul Allen** founded Microsoft in 1975, and their MS-DOS operating system became the standard for IBM PCs and compatibles. Microsoft's strategic licensing agreements and development of widely-used applications, such as Microsoft Word and Excel, positioned the company as a dominant force in the software industry. The launch of **Windows** in 1985, with its GUI, further solidified Microsoft's position, making personal computing more accessible and functional.

Conclusion

The microprocessor revolution fundamentally transformed the computing landscape, shrinking powerful computers down to a size and price that made them accessible to individuals and small businesses. The development of the microprocessor catalyzed the rise of personal computers, democratizing computing power and leading to an explosion of innovation and growth in the technology industry.

The contributions of companies like Intel, Apple, IBM, and Microsoft were pivotal in this era, each driving advancements that made computers more powerful, affordable, and user-friendly. This period set the stage for the digital age, as personal computers became indispensable tools for work, education, and entertainment.

As we continue our exploration of computing history,

the next chapters will delve into the rise of the Internet and networking, the era of portable computing, and the modern advances that have shaped the current technological landscape.

CHAPTER 6: THE INTERNET AND NETWORKING

The Origins of the Internet

The story of the Internet begins in the early days of computer networking, a period characterized by experimentation and innovation driven by the need to share information and resources across different machines. The roots of the Internet can be traced back to the 1960s, when the U.S. Department of Defense initiated a research project called ARPANET (Advanced Research Projects Agency Network).

ARPANET was conceived as a means to connect computers at various research institutions, enabling them to communicate and share data efficiently. In 1969, ARPANET achieved a major milestone with the successful transmission of a message between two nodes: one at UCLA and the other at the Stanford Research Institute. This event marked the birth of the first packet-switching network, a foundational technology that would underpin the Internet.

ARPANET and Early Networking Efforts

Packet-switching, developed by pioneers such as **Paul Baran** and **Donald Davies**, was a revolutionary concept that broke data into smaller packets that could be transmitted independently over a network and reassembled at the destination. This method was more efficient and reliable than traditional circuit-switching, as it allowed multiple communications to share the same network paths simultaneously.

Throughout the 1970s, ARPANET expanded rapidly, connecting more universities and research centers. This period also saw the development of key networking protocols, including the **Network Control Protocol (NCP)**, which facilitated communication between computers on the network.

A significant breakthrough came in 1973 when **Vint Cerf** and **Bob Kahn** proposed the **Transmission Control Protocol (TCP)**, which later evolved into the **Transmission Control Protocol/Internet Protocol (TCP/IP)**suite. TCP/IP provided a robust and scalable framework for network communication, enabling different types of networks to interconnect seamlessly. By 1983, TCP/IP became the standard protocol for ARPANET, laying the foundation for the modern Internet.

The Emergence of the World Wide Web

The 1980s and early 1990s witnessed the transformation of the Internet from a primarily academic and military tool into a global communication network accessible to the general public. A pivotal moment in this transition was the creation of the **World Wide Web (WWW)** by **Tim Berners-Lee** at CERN (the European Organization for Nuclear Research) in 1989.

Berners-Lee's invention introduced a system of interlinked hypertext documents accessible via the Internet, using browsers to navigate between them. The key components of the World Wide Web included:
- **HTML (Hypertext Markup Language)**: A standard language for creating and formatting web pages.
- **HTTP (Hypertext Transfer Protocol)**: A protocol for transferring hypertext requests and information on the web.
- **URLs (Uniform Resource Locators)**: Addresses used to locate and access web resources.

In 1993, the release of **Mosaic,** the first widely-used graphical web browser developed by **Marc Andreessen**and **Eric Bina** at the National Center for Supercomputing Applications (NCSA), made the Web more user-friendly and visually appealing. Mosaic's success spurred the growth of the Internet by making it accessible to a broader audience, leading to an explosion of websites and online content.

The Expansion and Commercialization of the Internet

The mid-1990s saw the commercialization of the Internet, with businesses and consumers increasingly embracing the new medium. The advent of commercial Internet Service Providers (ISPs) allowed individuals and companies to connect to the Internet more easily. Key milestones during this period included the founding of pioneering web companies such as **Amazon** (1994), **eBay** (1995), and **Google** (1998), which played crucial roles in shaping the digital economy.

Email, a key application of the Internet, became an essential tool for communication, while the rise of social media platforms like **Facebook** (2004) and **Twitter** (2006) transformed how people interact and share information.

The Impact of Networking Technologies

The evolution of the Internet has been driven by continuous advancements in networking technologies, which have significantly enhanced its speed, capacity, and reliability. Key developments include:
- **Broadband Internet**: The transition from dial-up to broadband connections in the early 2000s provided faster and more reliable Internet access, enabling richer multimedia content and more interactive online experiences.
- **Wireless Networking**: The proliferation of Wi-Fi and mobile networks (3G, 4G, and 5G) has made Internet access ubiquitous, supporting the growth of mobile computing and the Internet of Things (IoT).
- **Fiber Optics**: The deployment of fiber-optic cables has dramatically increased the bandwidth and speed of Internet connections, facilitating the growth of high-definition streaming, cloud computing, and other data-intensive applications.

Conclusion

The Internet and networking have revolutionized how we

live, work, and communicate, transforming virtually every aspect of modern society. From its origins in ARPANET and early networking efforts to the creation of the World Wide Web and the commercialization of the Internet, the journey has been marked by remarkable technological advancements and profound societal impacts.

As we look to the future, emerging technologies such as quantum networking, advanced cybersecurity measures, and the continued expansion of the IoT promise to drive further innovations and reshape the digital landscape once again.

In the following chapters, we will explore the era of portable computing, the advancements in artificial intelligence, and the continuous evolution of technology that continues to shape our world in profound ways.

CHAPTER 7: THE ERA OF PORTABLE COMPUTING

Introduction

The journey of computing took a significant turn with the advent of portable computing. As technology advanced, the desire for mobility and convenience led to the development of laptops, tablets, and smartphones. These devices revolutionized how we interact with technology, making computing power accessible on the go. This chapter explores the evolution of portable computing, examining its impact on society and the technological innovations that made it possible.

The Birth of Laptops

The concept of portable computing dates back to the early 1970s when engineers and inventors began experimenting with the idea of a computer that could be easily carried. The first commercially successful portable computer was the Osborne 1, released in 1981. Developed by Adam Osborne, the Osborne 1 featured a built-in screen, keyboard, and floppy disk drives. Despite its bulky design and weight of nearly 25 pounds, it set the stage for the development of more compact and user-friendly laptops.

The 1980s and 1990s saw significant advancements in laptop technology. Companies like IBM, Toshiba, and Apple played pivotal roles in refining and popularizing portable computers. IBM's ThinkPad series, introduced in 1992, became iconic for its robust design and innovative features, including the TrackPoint pointing stick. Apple's PowerBook, launched in 1991, set new standards for laptop design with its sleek form factor and ergonomic keyboard layout.

The Rise of Mobile Computing

As laptops became more powerful and affordable, the demand for even more portable and versatile devices grew. This demand led to the development of mobile computing devices, which combined the capabilities of computers with the convenience of handheld gadgets.

The introduction of Personal Digital Assistants (PDAs) in the 1990s marked an important step in this direction. Devices like the PalmPilot, released in 1997, allowed users to manage contacts, calendars, and tasks on a portable device. While limited in functionality compared to modern smartphones, PDAs laid the groundwork for the development of more advanced mobile computing devices.

The Advent of Tablets

Tablets emerged as a new category of portable computing devices, offering larger screens and touch-based interfaces. Microsoft's Tablet PC, introduced in 2002, was one of the first attempts to bring tablet computing to the mainstream. However, it was Apple's iPad, launched in 2010, that truly revolutionized the tablet market. With its intuitive touch interface, sleek design, and robust ecosystem of apps, the iPad quickly became a popular choice for both personal and professional use.

The success of the iPad spurred other companies to develop their own tablets, leading to a diverse market with options for various needs and preferences. Tablets became essential tools for education, entertainment, and productivity, further cementing the importance of portable computing in modern life.

The Smartphone Revolution

Perhaps the most transformative development in portable computing was the rise of the smartphone. Combining the features of a mobile phone, PDA, and computer, smartphones have become indispensable tools for communication, work, and entertainment.

The introduction of the iPhone by Apple in 2007 marked a turning point in the smartphone industry. The iPhone's revolutionary touch interface, robust operating system, and integration with the App Store set new standards for mobile devices. Competitors like Google, with its Android operating system, and Samsung quickly followed suit, leading to a rapid evolution of smartphone technology.

Smartphones have significantly impacted various aspects of daily life. They have transformed how we communicate, access information, and perform tasks. With powerful processors, high-resolution cameras, and a vast array of apps, smartphones have become essential tools for productivity, creativity, and entertainment.

Impact on Society

The era of portable computing has had profound implications for society. Laptops, tablets, and smartphones have made computing power accessible to a wider audience, breaking down barriers to information and communication. These devices have empowered individuals and businesses, enabling remote work, online education, and global connectivity.

Portable computing has also transformed industries. In healthcare, mobile devices facilitate telemedicine and remote patient monitoring. In education, tablets and laptops enhance learning experiences and provide access to digital resources. In business, mobile computing enables real-time collaboration and access to critical data from anywhere in the world.

Technological Innovations

Several technological advancements have driven the evolution of portable computing. Improvements in battery technology have extended the usage time of mobile devices, while advances in microprocessors have increased their computing power. Innovations in display technology have led to higher resolution screens and touch interfaces, enhancing user experiences.

Wireless connectivity has been another crucial factor in

the rise of portable computing. Wi-Fi, Bluetooth, and cellular networks enable seamless communication and data transfer, making it possible to stay connected on the go. The development of cloud computing has further enhanced the capabilities of portable devices, allowing users to access and store data remotely.

Conclusion

The era of portable computing has reshaped the technological landscape, bringing the power of computing into the palms of our hands. Laptops, tablets, and smartphones have revolutionized how we interact with technology, making it more accessible, convenient, and integral to our daily lives.

As we look to the future, the continued evolution of portable computing promises even more exciting developments. Emerging technologies such as foldable screens, augmented reality, and advanced artificial intelligence are poised to further transform the way we use and perceive portable devices.

In the next chapter, we will explore the advancements in artificial intelligence and machine learning, examining how these cutting-edge technologies are shaping the future of computing and beyond.

CHAPTER 8: MODERN COMPUTING AND BEYOND

Introduction

The field of computing has undergone a radical transformation since its inception, evolving from mechanical contraptions and vacuum tubes to sophisticated, highly integrated digital systems. As we enter the 21st century, computing continues to advance at a breathtaking pace, driven by breakthroughs in hardware, software, and new paradigms of computation. This chapter delves into the state of modern computing, exploring the latest innovations and envisioning the potential future directions of the field.

The Age of Supercomputers

Modern computing has been significantly shaped by the development of supercomputers—immensely powerful machines capable of performing billions or trillions of calculations per second. These machines tackle complex problems in scientific research, weather forecasting, cryptography, and more.

Supercomputers have grown exponentially in power and capability due to advances in parallel processing, where thousands of processors work simultaneously on different parts of a problem. Notable examples include the IBM Summit and the Chinese Sunway TaihuLight, which have reached previously unimaginable levels of performance. These machines are essential for tasks that require immense computational power, such as simulating nuclear reactions, analyzing vast genomic datasets, and modeling climate change.

Quantum Computing: The Next Frontier

One of the most promising areas in modern computing is quantum computing. Unlike classical computers, which use bits to process information as 0s or 1s, quantum computers use quantum bits, or qubits, which can represent and process multiple states simultaneously due to the principles of superposition and entanglement.

Quantum computing holds the potential to solve certain problems much faster than classical computers. For example, quantum algorithms could revolutionize fields such as cryptography, materials science, and complex system simulations. Companies like IBM, Google, and startups like Rigetti and D-Wave are making significant strides in developing practical quantum computers.

In 2019, Google claimed to have achieved "quantum supremacy" with its Sycamore processor, performing a specific computation faster than the world's fastest supercomputer could. While practical, large-scale quantum computing is still in its infancy, the progress made so far suggests a transformative future.

Artificial Intelligence and Machine Learning

Artificial intelligence (AI) and machine learning (ML) are among the most dynamic and rapidly evolving areas of modern computing. These technologies enable computers to learn from data and make decisions, mimicking cognitive functions such as perception, reasoning, and problem-solving.

AI and ML have found applications in numerous fields, including healthcare, finance, transportation, and entertainment. In healthcare, AI algorithms can diagnose diseases from medical images with remarkable accuracy. In finance, they detect fraudulent transactions and automate trading strategies. Autonomous vehicles rely on AI to navigate complex environments, and personalized recommendation systems enhance user experiences on platforms like Netflix and Amazon.

Deep learning, a subset of machine learning, has driven much of the recent progress in AI. Techniques such as convolutional neural networks (CNNs) and recurrent neural networks (RNNs) have enabled breakthroughs in image recognition, natural language processing, and speech synthesis. Innovations like OpenAI's GPT-4 have demonstrated the potential of AI to understand and generate human-like text, opening new possibilities for human-computer interaction.

Edge Computing and the Internet of Things (IoT)

As the number of connected devices grows, the Internet of Things (IoT) has become a critical component of modern computing. IoT encompasses a vast network of physical devices—ranging from household appliances to industrial machinery—embedded with sensors, software, and connectivity to exchange data.

To handle the massive influx of data generated by IoT devices, edge computing has emerged as a vital technology. Edge computing involves processing data closer to where it is generated, rather than relying solely on centralized cloud servers. This reduces latency, improves efficiency, and enables real-time analytics and decision-making.

Applications of IoT and edge computing are diverse and impactful. In smart cities, sensors monitor traffic patterns and optimize energy use. In agriculture, IoT devices track soil conditions and weather patterns to optimize crop yields. In manufacturing, edge computing enhances predictive maintenance and quality control.

Cloud Computing and Data Centers

Cloud computing has revolutionized the way organizations store, process, and access data. By offering scalable and flexible computing resources over the internet, cloud computing allows businesses to operate more efficiently and cost-effectively.

Major cloud service providers like Amazon Web Services (AWS), Microsoft Azure, and Google Cloud Platform dominate the market, offering a wide range of services, from storage and computing power to advanced AI and machine learning tools. These platforms enable companies to deploy applications quickly, scale resources according to demand, and leverage powerful analytics and big data solutions.

Modern data centers, which power cloud services, are marvels of engineering and efficiency. They utilize advanced cooling techniques, energy-efficient hardware, and sophisticated management software to ensure reliability and performance. Hyperscale data centers, operated by major tech companies, can house hundreds of thousands of servers and provide the backbone for the global digital economy.

Emerging Technologies and Future Directions

As we look beyond the present, several emerging technologies promise to further transform the landscape of computing:

- **Neuromorphic Computing**: Inspired by the structure and function of the human brain, neuromorphic computing aims to create hardware that can process information in a manner similar to biological neural networks. This could lead to more efficient and powerful AI systems.
- **5G and Beyond**: The rollout of 5G networks promises faster, more reliable, and low-latency wireless communication. This will enhance mobile computing, IoT, and enable new applications like augmented reality (AR) and virtual reality (VR).
- **Blockchain and Decentralized Computing**: Blockchain

technology offers a secure and transparent way to record transactions and data. It has applications beyond cryptocurrencies, including supply chain management, digital identity, and decentralized applications (DApps).

- **Extended Reality (XR)**: XR encompasses AR, VR, and mixed reality (MR). These technologies blend the physical and digital worlds, offering immersive experiences for gaming, training, healthcare, and remote collaboration.

Conclusion

Modern computing stands at the intersection of numerous technological advancements, each contributing to a more interconnected, intelligent, and efficient digital world. From the raw power of supercomputers and the potential of quantum computing to the transformative impact of AI and the ubiquity of IoT, the landscape of computing is continuously evolving.

As we move forward, the integration of these technologies will drive further innovations, shaping the future in ways we can only begin to imagine. The relentless pace of progress ensures that the story of computing is far from over. As we conclude this journey through the history and evolution of computers, we find ourselves at the dawn of a new era, where the possibilities are limitless and the future is being written in code and silicon.

In the next chapters, we will explore specific applications and case studies of these advanced technologies, delving deeper into how they are already changing the world and what we can expect in the coming years. The adventure of computing continues, and with it, the promise of an ever more connected and intelligent world.

✳✳✳✳✳✳

CHAPTER 9: THE SOCIAL AND CULTURAL IMPACT OF COMPUTERS

Introduction

The pervasive influence of computers extends far beyond their technological capabilities. They have reshaped societies, altered cultural norms, and redefined human interaction. As tools for communication, entertainment, education, and work, computers have become integral to modern life, influencing how we think, learn, and connect with one another. This chapter explores the profound social and cultural impact of computers, examining both the positive transformations and the challenges they present.

The Digital Divide

One of the most significant social issues associated with the rise of computers is the digital divide—the gap between those who have access to modern information and communication technology and those who do not. This divide can exist between different countries, regions, and even communities within the same country.

In developed nations, access to computers and the internet has become almost ubiquitous, fostering opportunities for education, employment, and social connectivity. However, in many developing regions, limited access to technology can exacerbate existing inequalities, restricting opportunities for advancement and participation in the global economy.

Efforts to bridge the digital divide have included initiatives to provide affordable devices, expand internet infrastructure, and implement digital literacy programs. Organizations and governments worldwide recognize that reducing this divide is crucial for fostering inclusive economic growth and social development.

Education and Learning

Computers have revolutionized education, transforming how knowledge is delivered and accessed. E-learning platforms, digital textbooks, and online courses have made education more flexible and accessible, breaking down geographical barriers and providing opportunities for lifelong learning.

Interactive and multimedia content can enhance understanding and engagement, making learning more effective. Tools such as educational games, simulations, and virtual labs provide hands-on experiences that were previously impossible in a traditional classroom setting.

Moreover, computers facilitate personalized learning

experiences. Adaptive learning technologies can tailor educational content to individual students' needs and learning paces, improving outcomes and fostering a more inclusive educational environment.

Work and Employment

The impact of computers on the workplace has been profound. Automation and digital tools have increased productivity, enabled remote work, and created new job opportunities while also rendering certain job roles obsolete.

The rise of telecommuting, accelerated by the COVID-19 pandemic, demonstrates the flexibility that computers and internet connectivity offer. Remote work tools, such as video conferencing software, project management platforms, and cloud services, have made it possible for teams to collaborate from anywhere in the world.

However, the shift towards a digital economy also poses challenges. Workers need to continuously update their skills to keep pace with technological advancements, and there is an increasing demand for digital literacy across all job sectors. The gig economy, facilitated by digital platforms, offers flexibility but also raises questions about job security and workers' rights.

Communication and Social Interaction

Computers and the internet have dramatically changed how we communicate and socialize. Social media platforms, instant messaging apps, and video conferencing tools allow us to connect with others instantly, regardless of distance.

These technologies have created new forms of social interaction and community-building. Social media enables individuals to share their lives, express opinions, and engage with a global audience. Online communities bring together people with shared interests, providing support networks and fostering collaboration.

However, the digital age has also introduced challenges. The prevalence of social media can contribute to issues such as cyberbullying, privacy concerns, and the spread of misinformation. The nature of online interactions, often characterized by brevity and anonymity, can sometimes lead to misunderstandings and a lack of empathy.

Entertainment and Media

The entertainment industry has been transformed by computers, from how content is created to how it is consumed. Digital media, including streaming services, online gaming, and social media platforms, offer unprecedented access to entertainment and have reshaped the cultural landscape.

The rise of streaming services like Netflix, Spotify, and YouTube has revolutionized how we consume movies, music, and videos. These platforms provide on-demand access to vast libraries of content, changing viewing and listening habits and challenging traditional media distribution models.

In the gaming industry, advancements in computer graphics and processing power have led to immersive experiences, blurring the lines between reality and virtual worlds. Online gaming communities bring together players from around the globe, creating new social dynamics and cultural phenomena.

Cultural Preservation and Innovation

Computers have also played a crucial role in cultural preservation and innovation. Digital archives and online museums make it possible to preserve and share cultural heritage, ensuring that future generations can access historical documents, artworks, and artifacts.

At the same time, technology has spurred cultural innovation. Digital art, virtual reality experiences, and interactive storytelling are just a few examples of how artists and creators are leveraging technology to push the boundaries of expression and creativity. The internet serves as a global stage, allowing diverse voices to be heard and fostering cross-cultural exchange.

Ethical and Privacy Concerns

The widespread use of computers and digital technologies raises important ethical and privacy concerns. Issues such as data privacy, surveillance, and the ethical use of artificial intelligence are increasingly at the forefront of public discourse.

Data privacy is a critical concern as individuals' personal information is collected, stored, and analyzed on a massive scale. The rise of big data analytics and the monetization of personal data by companies have sparked debates about user consent, data protection, and the right to privacy.

Surveillance technologies, facilitated by advanced computing systems, pose challenges to civil liberties. Governments and organizations have the ability to monitor and track individuals' activities, raising concerns about abuse of power and the erosion of privacy.

The ethical use of artificial intelligence and automation also presents significant challenges. Questions about bias in AI algorithms, accountability for autonomous systems, and the societal impact of job displacement due to automation are complex issues that require careful consideration and regulation.

Conclusion

The social and cultural impact of computers is vast and multifaceted, encompassing profound transformations in how we live, work, communicate, and entertain ourselves. While computers have brought about significant advancements and opportunities, they have also introduced new challenges and ethical dilemmas.

As we navigate the digital age, it is crucial to address these challenges thoughtfully and inclusively, ensuring that the benefits of technology are accessible to all and that ethical considerations guide its development and use. By doing so, we can harness the power of computers to create a more connected, informed, and equitable   society.

In the next chapter, we will explore the environmental impact of computing and the sustainability challenges and opportunities associated with our increasingly digital world.

CHAPTER 10: CONCLUSION: REFLECTING ON THE JOURNEY

Introduction

As we come to the conclusion of our exploration into the origin and evolution of computers, it's essential to reflect on the incredible journey we've traversed. From the ancient tools of calculation to the sophisticated digital systems of today, computers have transformed our world in ways that were once unimaginable. This chapter looks back on the key milestones, innovations, and individuals that have shaped computing history and contemplates the future directions of this dynamic field.

The Evolutionary Milestones

The history of computing is marked by several pivotal milestones, each representing a significant leap forward in technology and human ingenuity.

1. Early Mechanical Computers:
   - The journey began with mechanical devices

like the abacus and the Antikythera mechanism, which demonstrated the human desire to automate calculation and record-keeping.

2. The Age of Electronic Computers:
  - The mid-20th century saw the development of the first electronic computers, such as ENIAC and UNIVAC. These machines, though massive and power-hungry, laid the groundwork for modern computing.

3. The Microprocessor Revolution:
  - The invention of the microprocessor in the 1970s by companies like Intel revolutionized computing, leading to the development of personal computers that brought computing power to homes and small businesses.

4. The Rise of the Internet:
  - The advent of the Internet in the late 20th century connected the world in unprecedented ways, transforming how we access information, communicate, and conduct business.

5. The Era of Portable Computing:
  - The development of laptops, tablets, and smartphones in the late 20th and early 21st centuries made computing portable and ubiquitous, changing how we work, learn, and interact.

6. Advances in Artificial Intelligence and Machine Learning:
  - Recent advancements in AI and ML have opened new frontiers in computing, enabling machines to learn from data and perform tasks that previously required human

intelligence.

Key Innovators and Visionaries

Throughout the history of computing, numerous individuals have made significant contributions that have shaped the field. Their vision, creativity, and perseverance have driven technological progress and inspired future generations.

1. Charles Babbage and Ada Lovelace:
   - Charles Babbage conceptualized the first mechanical computer, the Analytical Engine, while Ada Lovelace is celebrated as the first computer programmer for her work on Babbage's machine.

2. Alan Turing:
   - Alan Turing's theoretical work laid the foundations of computer science and artificial intelligence. His contributions to breaking the Enigma code during World War II also had a profound impact on the development of early computers.

3. John von Neumann:
   - John von Neumann's architecture for computer design, which includes a central processing unit and stored program concept, remains the foundation of most modern computers.

4. Bill Gates and Steve Jobs:

- Bill Gates and Steve Jobs were pivotal in popularizing personal computing. Gates, through Microsoft, made software widely accessible, while Jobs, through Apple, revolutionized the design and user experience of personal devices.

Societal Transformations

Computers have not only transformed technology but also profoundly impacted society and culture. They have reshaped industries, influenced education, altered communication, and even changed how we perceive the world.

1. Education:
- Computers and the internet have democratized access to knowledge, providing educational resources to millions worldwide and fostering lifelong learning.

2. Communication:
- The advent of social media, email, and instant messaging has changed how we communicate, making it faster and more accessible, but also raising issues around privacy and the quality of interactions.

3. Work:
- The digital revolution has transformed the workplace, enabling remote work, increasing productivity, and creating new job roles while also posing challenges like job displacement due to automation.

4. Entertainment:
- The way we consume and create entertainment

has been revolutionized by digital media, online gaming, and streaming services, creating new cultural norms and economic models.

Future Directions

As we look to the future, the field of computing continues to evolve, presenting new challenges and opportunities.

1. Quantum Computing:
- Quantum computing promises to solve complex problems that are currently intractable for classical computers, potentially revolutionizing fields like cryptography, materials science, and complex system simulations.

2. Artificial Intelligence:
- AI continues to advance, with potential applications ranging from autonomous vehicles to personalized medicine. Ethical considerations and governance will be crucial as AI becomes more integrated into society.

3. Sustainability:
- The environmental impact of computing, including energy consumption and electronic waste, is a growing concern. Innovations in green computing and sustainable practices will be vital for the future.

4. Human-Computer Interaction:
- Emerging technologies such as augmented reality (AR), virtual reality (VR), and brain-computer interfaces are poised to transform how we interact with machines, blending the physical and digital worlds.

Conclusion

The history of computers is a testament to human creativity, perseverance, and the relentless pursuit of progress. From the earliest mechanical calculators to the cutting-edge technologies of today, each advancement has built upon the work of those who came before, pushing the boundaries of what is possible.

As we reflect on this journey, it is clear that the story of computing is far from over. The innovations and challenges that lie ahead will continue to shape our world in profound ways. By understanding the past and contemplating the future, we can appreciate the remarkable achievements of computing and the endless possibilities that await us.

In this ever-evolving field, one thing remains constant: the drive to explore, innovate, and harness the power of technology to improve our lives and connect our world. The journey of computing is a continuous adventure, and we are all participants in writing its next chapter.

[Shreyan Hait]
[24-05-2024]

ABOUT THE AUTHOR

Shreyan Hait

I'm Shreyan Hait, a writer fascinated by the intersection of technology and human nature. My stories explore mature, thought-provoking themes, delving into how innovation shapes our emotions, relationships, and identities. A passionate gamer and tech enthusiast, I draw inspiration from immersive digital worlds and cutting-edge advancements, weaving these elements into speculative narratives that challenge and captivate. Through my work, I invite readers to imagine futures where the lines between human and machine blur, sparking reflection on the ever-evolving role of technology in our lives.

EPILOGUE

As we close the pages on this exploration of the origin and evolution of computers, it's worth taking a moment to reflect on the remarkable journey we've charted. From the humble beginnings of mechanical calculation devices to the sophisticated and interconnected digital world of today, the history of computing is a story of human ingenuity, perseverance, and relentless pursuit of progress.

The Enduring Legacy of Computing

The evolution of computers is not merely a chronicle of technological advancements but a testament to the profound impact these innovations have on every aspect of our lives. The devices we now take for granted—our smartphones, laptops, and smart appliances—are the culmination of centuries of innovation, each breakthrough building upon the last.

This journey has not been without its challenges and setbacks. The path of progress is often winding, marked by both triumphant achievements and obstacles that required overcoming immense technical and conceptual hurdles. Yet, each challenge surmounted has only fueled further advancements, driving us toward greater heights.

A World Transformed

Computers have fundamentally transformed the way we live, work, and interact. They have democratized access to information, bridged distances, and created a global community interconnected in ways previously unimaginable. From revolutionizing industries and driving economic growth to enabling groundbreaking scientific discoveries and fostering social change, the influence of computers is pervasive and profound.

In education, healthcare, entertainment, and beyond, the applications of computing continue to expand, reshaping our world and opening new possibilities. The digital age has brought with it opportunities for innovation and collaboration that transcend borders and cultural divides, fostering a global exchange of ideas and knowledge.

The Road Ahead

As we stand on the cusp of new technological frontiers, it is clear that the story of computing is far from over. Emerging technologies such as quantum computing, artificial intelligence, and the Internet of Things promise to drive the next wave of innovation, presenting both exciting possibilities and complex challenges. The future of computing will undoubtedly be shaped by our ability to harness these technologies responsibly and ethically.

The questions we face today—about privacy, security, ethical AI, and sustainability—are critical in shaping the trajectory of future advancements. As we move forward, it is essential to consider not only the technological potential but also the societal implications of these innovations.

Gratitude and Inspiration

This journey through the history of computing is a tribute to the countless visionaries, engineers, scientists, and dreamers who have dedicated their lives to pushing the boundaries of what is possible. Their contributions have laid the foundation for the digital age and continue to inspire new generations of innovators.

To the readers of this book, my hope is that this exploration has not only provided a deeper understanding of the technological evolution but also sparked curiosity and appreciation for the incredible achievements of the past and the boundless potential of the future.

A Continuation

The narrative of computing is a continuous story, written by each discovery, innovation, and application that builds upon the last. As technology continues to evolve, so too does our capacity to shape and redefine the world around us. The journey is ongoing, and each of us plays a part in it.

In closing, let us carry forward the spirit of innovation and curiosity that has driven the history of computing. As we look to the future, may we strive to create technology that enriches lives, bridges divides, and fosters a more connected, equitable, and sustainable world. The adventure of computing is an endless one, and it is ours to continue.

[Shreyan Hait]
[24-05-2024]

AFTERWORD

Writing this book has been a journey in itself—a journey through time, technology, and the incredible human spirit of innovation. As I conclude, I am filled with a deep sense of gratitude for the pioneers who have shaped the field of computing and the countless individuals who continue to push its boundaries.

Reflections on Writing

Exploring the vast expanse of computing history has been both enlightening and humbling. The story of computers is not just about machines and algorithms; it is about the people who dared to dream and the societies that were transformed by those dreams. Each chapter in this book has sought to capture the essence of these transformative moments, from the ancient abacuses to the latest in quantum computing.

The writing process has reinforced my appreciation for the interconnectedness of technological advancements and societal progress. As I delved into the lives of innovators like Charles Babbage, Ada Lovelace, Alan Turing, and many others, I realized that their contributions were not merely technical but profoundly human. Their work was driven by curiosity, creativity, and a desire to solve complex problems —traits that are as important today as they were centuries ago.

Acknowledgments

I owe a great deal of gratitude to many people who supported and inspired me throughout the writing of this book. To my family and friends, thank you for your unwavering encouragement and patience. Your belief in this project kept me motivated even during the most challenging moments.

I would also like to thank my colleagues and mentors in the field of computer science and technology. Your insights, feedback, and shared passion for computing have been invaluable. Special thanks to those who reviewed early drafts of the manuscript and provided critical feedback.

Looking Forward

As we look to the future, it is clear that the landscape of computing will continue to evolve in ways we cannot fully predict. The rapid pace of technological change presents both opportunities and challenges. It is up to us to harness these advancements ethically and responsibly, ensuring that they benefit all of humanity.

The next chapters in the story of computing will be written by those who dare to innovate and think beyond the conventional. Whether you are a student, a professional, or an enthusiast, your contributions matter. The field of computing thrives on diverse perspectives and the collaborative effort to solve problems and create new possibilities.

A Call to Action

I hope this book has inspired you to explore the world of computing further, to appreciate its history, and to engage with its future. Whether you are coding your first program, designing a new piece of hardware, or simply using technology in your daily life, remember that you are part of a long and proud tradition of innovation.

Let us continue to ask questions, seek answers, and build tools that make the world a better place. The journey of computing is far from over, and it is up to each of us to shape its future.

Final Thoughts

In the grand narrative of human progress, computers have played a pivotal role, transforming our world in profound and lasting ways. As we close this book, we do so with the understanding that the story of computing is a living, breathing entity—constantly evolving, growing, and adapting.

Thank you for joining me on this journey. May it inspire you to explore, innovate, and contribute to the ever-expanding field of computing.

[Shreyan Hait]
[24-05-2024]

ACKNOWLEDGEMENT

Writing this book has been an incredible journey, and it would not have been possible without the support, encouragement, and insights of many wonderful people. I am deeply grateful to everyone who has contributed to the completion of this project.

First and foremost, I would like to thank my family. Your unwavering support and understanding have been my bedrock throughout this endeavor.

I am also indebted to the many pioneers of computing whose stories fill these pages. While I have never met many of you, your work and dedication have profoundly influenced my understanding of the field. This book is as much a tribute to your achievements as it is an exploration of the technology you helped create.

Finally, I would like to thank my readers. Your curiosity and passion for understanding the evolution of computing inspire me. It is for you that this book was written, and I hope it serves as a source of knowledge, inspiration, and wonder.

To everyone who has been a part of this journey, whether mentioned here or not, please know that your contributions have been deeply appreciated. This book is a collective effort, and I am grateful for your support.

Thank you.
[Shreyan Hait]
[24-05-2024]

SPECIAL OFFER

Every book I write the first 200 copies are always discounted at a very low price to get it contact on my email account and ask for the book if you are selected the dicounted price will be sent just give your complete address.

Email :- goddevilbooks@gmail.com

Thank you For supporting ,
Shreyan Hait
[Author]